AF322609

B. VINCENT

---

10 STEPS TO A POWERFUL PERSONAL BRAND

STAND OUT AND SUCCEED

QuantumQuill Press

CONTENTS

INTRODUCTION

Determining Personal Branding: In the contemporary era characterized by rapidity and intense competition, personal branding has surfaced as an indispensable element for attaining success. Personal branding incorporates not only the development of an attention-grabbing logo or a poignant tagline, but also an authentic reflection of one's identity, values, and public persona. It is the intentional and strategic process of influencing the personal and professional perceptions of others. Your personal brand consists of a singular fusion of your accomplishments, strengths, values, and aspirations, which distinguish you from others in your industry. By comprehending and delineating one's personal brand, one acquires lucidity regarding one's identity, objective, and trajectory, thereby establishing a robust groundwork for the attainment of objectives and differentiation amidst a saturated market. In this book, we shall explore the intricacies of personal branding in greater detail and furnish you with practical strategies to develop a robust and genuine brand that connects with your target audience and drives your achievements. Consequently, let us commence this paradigm-shifting expedition by initially comprehending the profound significance of personal branding and its indispensable nature for both one's personal and professional development.

The significance of personal branding becomes apparent when attempting to distinguish oneself amidst the vast ocean of entrepreneurs and professionals. However, in a society where attention is limited, establishing a robust personal brand is not merely an option; it is an essential. Your personal brand functions as a representation of your reputation, calling card, and commitment to the world. It is what establishes a unique market position, facilitates access to untapped prospects, and differentiates you as an authority in your field. In addition to attracting clients, collaborators, and career advancements, a skillfully constructed personal brand can inspire audience confidence and establish credibility. In addition to fostering professional achievement, personal branding establishes a connection between one's actions and their true selves, promoting a sense of satisfaction and authenticity. Fundamentally, personal branding grants you the ability to dictate your own story, influence others' perceptions, and make an enduring impact on all those you cross paths with. Remain mindful that as we commence this collaborative endeavor, allocating resources towards your personal brand signifies more than mere self-promotion; it fosters self-empowerment and establishes an enduring heritage that authentically embodies your essence. Therefore, let us delve into the profound impact that personal branding can have and unveil the boundless opportunities it presents for your forthcoming achievements.

The Ten-Step Structure: This literary work contains a strategic guide for constructing a formidable personal brand—one that exudes genuineness, lucidity, and influence. Through each phase of the personal branding voyage, our ten-step framework is intended to furnish you with practical strategies, thought-provoking exercises, and actionable insights. Every stage of the process, including establishing your brand identity, capitalizing on online platforms, networking efficiently, and refining your expertise, has been meticulously designed to assist you in attaining your utmost capabilities and distinguishing yourself amidst a saturated market. By employing this methodical approach, one can establish a clear trajectory to adhere to, facilitating systematic progress and enabling the implementation of progress evaluation. Whether you are an established professional aiming to elevate your brand or an aspiring entrepreneur trying to establish your niche, this framework can be modified to suit your specific objectives and situation. Therefore, as we commence this mutually transformative expedition, have faith in the process, welcome the obstacles that may arise, and envision the formidable personal brand that looms ahead. Let us commence and undertake the initial stride towards actualizing our utmost capabilities.

Reasons Why This Book Is Significant: You may be wondering, in a world flooded with self-help guides and online tutorials, what distinguishes this book. The solution can be found in its comprehensive methodology, pragmatic observations, and implementable tactics customized explicitly for constructing a formidable personal brand. In contrast to general guidance that guarantees immediate results and instantaneous prosperity, this book presents an all-encompassing plan that is firmly rooted in empirical investigation, practical knowledge, and tangible instances. It is not enough to simply discuss theory; concrete outcomes are also crucial. Furthermore, it is acknowledged in this book that personal branding is not a universally applicable undertaking. Whether you identify as an introvert, extrovert, freelancer, or corporate professional, the principles delineated in this article possess the flexibility to accommodate your distinct personality, situation, and objectives. By devoting your time and effort to reading this book, you are making a financial investment in your future self. You are embarking on a transformative, growth-oriented, and self-discovery journey—one that may significantly impact your life, relationships, and professional trajectory. Therefore, if you are prepared to advance towards reaching your utmost capabilities and distinguishing yourself in a competitive environment, this book serves as your reliable companion throughout that process. Together, we shall commence this endeavor and harness the potential of your personal brand.

Prompt for Action: Having established the foundation and framework for your personal branding endeavor, the present moment demands that you initiate the process. While perusing the forthcoming chapters, I urge you to approach every concept with a receptive mindset and a readiness to confront your limitations. In light of your personal journey, strengths, and ambitions, evaluate the extent to which they correspond with the principles expounded in this literary work. It is the practical implementation of that knowledge, not mere acquisition, that drives significant transformation. Therefore, upon encountering practical strategies and intellectually stimulating exercises, do not merely absorb them passively; actively participate in them, integrate them into your routine. Every action you undertake, such as honing your brand narrative, optimizing your digital footprint, or broadening your social circle, advances your trajectory toward actualizing your utmost capabilities and constructing a formidable personal brand. Even if you experience discouragement or overwhelming feelings along the path, keep in mind that you are not alone. Consult with colleagues, mentors, or the author themselves for assistance and direction. We can surpass any obstacle and accomplish amazing things when we unite. Therefore, armed with unwavering resolve and fortitude, we shall commence this paradigm-shifting expedition and release the complete potential of your personal brand. Your future self is eagerly awaiting your commencement at this moment.

CHAPTER 1: UNDERSTANDING PERSONAL BRANDING

What is Private Marking?

Individual marking, in its embodiment, is the conscious and vital development of your remarkable character and notoriety. It goes past simple self-advancement or promoting strategies; it's about really exhibiting what your identity is, a big motivator for you, and what makes you unmistakable in a jam-packed commercial center. Your own image incorporates your qualities, interests, abilities, and encounters, embodying the quintessence of your expert and individual excursion. It's the story you enlighten the world concerning yourself, the impression you have on others, and the inheritance you seek to make. Understanding individual marking includes perceiving the force of discernment and the significance of deliberate correspondence in forming how others see you. By embracing individual marking, you assume command over your story, separate yourself from the opposition, and cut out an extraordinary space in your industry or field. In this part, we dive further into the central ideas of individual marking, laying the preparation for your excursion towards building a strong and credible brand that resounds with your crowd.

The Advancement of Individual Marking

The idea of individual marking has navigated an entrancing transformative excursion, transforming from a generally dark thought to a foundation of current expert turn of events. Its underlying foundations can be followed back to old human advancements, where people utilized images, titles, and notorieties to separate themselves inside their networks. Nonetheless, it was only after the late twentieth century that individual marking started to take on its contemporary structure, prodded by the ascent of broad communications, globalization, and the computerized age.

In the computerized time, individual marking has become more open and unavoidable than any time in recent memory, because of the expansion of web-based entertainment stages, web based systems administration destinations, and individual sites. People presently have phenomenal open doors to organize their web-based personas, draw in with a worldwide crowd, and shape their expert personalities progressively.

In addition, the democratization of data and the gig economy have additionally pushed the significance of individual marking. In the present interconnected world, people are not generally limited by conventional vocation ways or authoritative progressive systems. All things being equal, they're engaged to construct their brands, seek after their interests, and make their fates based on their conditions.

Understanding the development of individual marking is critical for exploring its intricacies and bridling its likely in the advanced age. By following its authentic direction, we gain significant bits of knowledge into the hidden standards, patterns, and powers driving its proceeded with development. In this part, we investigate the critical achievements and changes that have molded individual marking into the strong peculiarity it is today, making way for your own marking process.

Why Individual Marking Matters

Individual marking isn't simply a popular expression or a brief pattern; it's an essential basic for outcome in the present serious scene. Whether you're a business visionary, a consultant, a corporate expert, or an imaginative craftsman, your own image assumes a crucial part in molding your vocation direction, drawing in open doors, and impacting how others see you.

In the computerized age, where data is plentiful and capacities to focus are temporary, individual marking fills in as an amazing asset for slicing through the clamor and establishing a noteworthy connection. It permits you to separate yourself from the opposition, exhibit your mastery, and secure yourself as a confided in expert in your field.

Also, individual marking isn't bound to proficient undertakings alone; it penetrates each part of your life, from your social collaborations to your own connections. By developing areas of strength for a brand, you upgrade your expert possibilities as well as develop a feeling of legitimacy, reason, and satisfaction.

Besides, in an undeniably interconnected world, where organizations and connections are vital, individual marking fills in as an impetus for building significant associations and encouraging joint effort. It permits you to explain your interesting incentive, impart your story, and produce veritable associations with similar people who share your qualities and desires.

Eventually, individual marking matters since it engages you to assume command over your account, shape your insight, and open your maximum capacity. It's not just about self-advancement or vanity; it's tied in with claiming your story, enhancing your effect, and leaving an enduring heritage that moves others.

In this part, we dive further into the horde justifications for why individual marking matters and investigate its significant ramifications for your expert and self-improvement. By understanding the meaning of individual marking, you'll be better prepared to outfit its power and influence it to accomplish your objectives and desires.

Fantasies and Misguided Judgments

Similarly as with any idea acquiring prevalence, individual marking is frequently encircled by fantasies and confusions that can impede its comprehension and execution. It's significant to disperse these misinterpretations to completely get a handle on the genuine substance and capability of individual marking.

One normal legend is that individual marking is just for big names or powerhouses with enormous followings. Truly, individual marking is pertinent to people at all levels and in all businesses. Whether you're a growing business visionary, a carefully prepared chief, or a new alumni entering the labor force, individual marking can essentially influence your expert direction and valuable open doors.

Another misinterpretation is that individual marking is inauthentic or egotistical. While it is actually the case that individual marking includes self-advancement somewhat, there's really no need to focus on gloating or overstating your accomplishments. Legitimate individual marking is established in mindfulness, straightforwardness, and certified association with your crowd. It's tied in with displaying your extraordinary assets and values in a manner that impacts others and enhances their lives.

Moreover, certain individuals accept that individual marking is a one-time exertion or a convenient solution for professional success. Notwithstanding, individual marking is a continuous cycle that requires consistency, exertion, and variation to develop with changing conditions and objectives. It's anything but a static personality yet a powerful story that develops and develops after some time.

Ultimately, there's a misguided judgment that individual marking is exclusively centered around online presence or virtual entertainment. While computerized stages assume a pivotal part in private marking, it's not the sole determinant of your image. Individual marking envelops different touchpoints, remembering for individual cooperations, proficient disposition, and local area commitment. It's tied in with making a firm and legitimate brand insight across all channels, both on the web and disconnected.

In this part, we expose these legends and misguided judgments encompassing individual marking, giving clearness and understanding to engage you on your marking process. By dispersing these fantasies, you'll be better prepared to embrace the genuine quintessence of individual marking and influence it to accomplish your expert and individual yearnings.

Distinguishing Your Remarkable Incentive

At the center of individual marking lies your remarkable offer — the particular mix of characteristics, abilities, and encounters that separates you from others in your field. Recognizing and articulating your exceptional offer is fundamental for building a convincing individual brand that reverberates with your crowd and separates you from the opposition.

To start this interaction, set aside some margin for thoughtfulness and self-reflection. Think about your assets, interests, and specialized topics. What are the abilities or characteristics that you succeed at? What special viewpoint or understanding do you offer that would be useful? Ponder your previous encounters, achievements, and difficulties. How have they molded who you are today and affected your expert process?

Then, think about your main interest group and their requirements, inclinations, and trouble spots. What issues or difficulties do they face, and what might you do for tackle them? How might you add worth and have a significant effect in their lives or professions? By understanding your crowd's requirements and adjusting your offer to their needs, you can tailor your own image to really impact them.

Whenever you've acquired lucidity on your interesting incentive, it's fundamental to convey it obviously and reliably across the entirety of your own marking touchpoints. Whether it's your LinkedIn profile, proficient bio, or brief presentation, guarantee that your informing mirrors your remarkable assets and the worth you deal to your crowd.

By distinguishing your novel offer, you not just lay out serious areas of strength for a for your own image yet additionally gain trust in your capacities and course. You become more purposeful and key in your profession choices, knowing how to use your assets and chances to accomplish your objectives. In this part, we'll dive further into the most common way of distinguishing and refining your special offer, outfitting you with the devices and bits of knowledge you want to construct a strong and true private brand.

CHAPTER 2: CLARIFYING YOUR BRAND IDENTITY

Characterizing Your Image Personality

At the core of individual marking lies an unmistakable and valid brand character — an outflow of what your identity is, what you worth, and what separates you from others. Characterizing your image character is a basic move toward the individual marking process, as it fills in as the directing light for all your marking endeavors.

To start, pause for a minute to consider your basic beliefs, convictions, and standards. What drives you? What makes the biggest difference to you in both your own and proficient life? Your qualities structure the bedrock of your image character, forming your activities, choices, and collaborations with others.

Then, think about your interests and interests. What exercises or subjects stimulate and rouse you? What do you very much want to do in your available energy? Your interests give important bits of knowledge into your legitimate self and can assist you with revealing remarkable parts of your image personality.

Moreover, ponder your drawn out objectives and goals. Where do you see yourself in five or a decade? What inheritance would you like to abandon? Your objectives can illuminate your image character by featuring the characteristics and qualities you really want to develop to make your vision of progress.

By incorporating these components — your qualities, interests, and objectives — you can start to create an unmistakable and convincing brand character that reverberates with who you are at your center. Your image character ought to be true, optimistic, and vital, mirroring the quintessence of what your identity is and a big motivator for you.

In this part, we'll dig further into the most common way of characterizing your image character, giving viable activities and experiences to assist you with uncovering the exceptional aspects of your own image. By explaining your image character, you'll establish a strong starting point for building a strong and bona fide individual brand that resounds with your crowd and separates you in a packed commercial center.

Making Your Image Story

Your image story is something beyond a story; it's the close to home center of your own image — the string that winds around together your encounters, values, and goals into a strong and convincing story. Making your image story is a groundbreaking cycle that permits you to verbalize what your identity is, a big motivator for you, and why you do what you do in a manner that resounds with your crowd on a more profound level.

To start making your image story, begin by pondering your own excursion — the urgent minutes, difficulties, and wins that have molded who you are today. What encounters fundamentally affect your life and vocation? How have these encounters impacted your qualities, convictions, and objectives?

Then, think about your extraordinary point of view and perspective. What bits of knowledge or examples have you acquired from your encounters? What do you offer of real value that no other person does? Your viewpoint separates you from others and makes your image story convincing and appealing.

As you make your image story, endeavor to be valid, defenseless, and interesting. Share your triumphs as well as your disappointments, misfortunes, and snapshots of development. Your crowd will resound with your mankind and realness, cultivating further associations and trust.

Also, consider the profound effect you believe that your image story should have on your crowd. What feelings would you like to summon? Whether it's motivation, compassion, or trust, injecting your image story with feeling will make it more paramount and effective.

At last, recall that your image story is a developing story — a no nonsense articulation of your own image. As you develop and advance, so too will your image story. Embrace the excursion of self-revelation and self-articulation, and let your image story be an impression of your bona fide self.

In this section, we'll dig further into the specialty of making your image story, giving viable tips, activities, and guides to assist you with articulating your remarkable account. By making a convincing brand story, you'll make a strong association with your crowd and raise your own image higher than ever.

Laying out Brand Consistency

Consistency is vital to building areas of strength for a conspicuous individual brand. It's tied in with guaranteeing that each part of your image — from your web-based presence to your correspondence style to your visual character — mirrors similar qualities, informing, and character. Laying out brand consistency improves your validity and incredible skill as well as supports your image's personality and reinforces your association with your crowd.

Perhaps the earliest move toward laying out brand consistency is characterizing your image components — like your logo, variety range, typography, and manner of speaking. These components act as the structure blocks of your image character and give a firm system to your marking endeavors.

Then, guarantee consistency across the entirety of your own marking touchpoints, both on the web and disconnected. This incorporates your site, virtual entertainment profiles, business cards, email marks, and some other materials or stages where your image is addressed. Utilize steady marking components, symbolism, and informing to make a brought together brand insight for your crowd.

Also, keep up with consistency in your correspondence style and manner of speaking. Whether you're composing a blog entry, sending an email, or giving a show, guarantee that your informing is lined up with your image values and character. Steady correspondence assembles trust and knowledge of your crowd, making them bound to draw in with and recall your image.

Consistency additionally stretches out to your way of behaving and activities. Be aware of how you introduce yourself in proficient settings, both on the web and disconnected. Your activities ought to line up with your image esteems and support the picture you need to pass on to your crowd.

At last, routinely screen and review your image consistency to guarantee that it stays in salvageable shape over the long haul. Direct occasional surveys of your marking materials, online profiles, and informing to distinguish any irregularities or regions for development. By keeping up with watchfulness and scrupulousness, you can maintain the respectability of your image and reinforce your association with your crowd.

In this section, we'll investigate the significance of laying out brand consistency and give pragmatic techniques and tips to keeping a firm and convincing individual brand. By focusing on consistency in your marking endeavors, you'll fabricate trust, validity, and acknowledgment with your crowd, making way for long haul achievement and effect.

Examining Your Ongoing Image Picture

Before you can refine and fortify your own image, it's fundamental to have a reasonable comprehension of your ongoing image picture. Directing a brand review permits you to survey how you're at present seen by your crowd, distinguish regions for development, and adjust your marking endeavors to your objectives and values.

Begin by assessing your internet based presence, including your site, online entertainment profiles, and whatever other computerized stages where your image is addressed. Think about the consistency of your marking components, the nature of your substance, and the commitment levels with your crowd. Focus on how your crowd cooperates with your image on the web and accumulate input to acquire experiences into their discernments and inclinations.

Then, evaluate your disconnected presence, including your expert attitude, organizing associations, and individual marking materials. Consider how you introduce yourself in proficient settings, the impression you have on others, and the arrangement between your disconnected way of behaving and your image values.

As you direct your image review, tell the truth and objective in your evaluation. Search for regions where your image might be conflicting, obsolete, or not completely lined up with your objectives and values. Recognize any qualities, shortcomings, amazing open doors, and dangers to your image's picture and notoriety.

Whenever you've finished your image review, examine the discoveries and focus on regions for development. Foster a strategy to address any holes or irregularities in your image picture, zeroing in on regions where you can have the main effect. This might include refreshing your marking materials, refining your informing, or improving your web-based presence.

At last, proceed to screen and assess your image picture routinely to guarantee that it stays lined up with your objectives and values. Lead occasional brand reviews to keep tabs on your development, recognize arising patterns, and make changes on a case by case basis to remain pertinent and serious in your industry.

In this section, we'll direct you through the most common way of reviewing your ongoing image picture, giving reasonable tips and apparatuses to assist you with surveying your image's assets and shortcomings. By directing a careful brand review, you'll acquire significant bits of knowledge into your image's discernment and position yourself for better progress in your own marking process.

Laying out Brand Objectives

Laying out clear and significant objectives is fundamental for directing your own marking endeavors and estimating your advancement enroute. Your image objectives act as the guide for your own marking process, giving guidance, concentration, and inspiration to accomplish your ideal results.

Begin by characterizing your all-encompassing brand objectives — what do you expect to accomplish with your own marking endeavors? Whether it's structure your web-based presence, extending your organization, or situating yourself as a specialist in your field, articulate your drawn out desires and goals.

Then, separate your overall image objectives into more modest, reachable achievements or targets. These achievements ought to be explicit, quantifiable, feasible, important, and time-bound (Savvy), permitting you to keep tabs on your development and praise your triumphs enroute.

Think about the different elements of your own image — like your internet based presence, organizing endeavors, proficient turn of events, and local area commitment — and distinguish explicit objective

CHAPTER 3: BUILDING YOUR ONLINE PRESENCE

Upgrading Your Web-based Entertainment Profiles

In the present computerized age, your web-based entertainment profiles act as the front way to your own image. They are in many cases the initial feeling that expected businesses, clients, or associates have of you, making it vital to advance them to line up with your own marking objectives.

Begin by evaluating and refreshing your profile data to guarantee it precisely mirrors your image personality. This incorporates your profile picture, cover photograph, bio, and some other pertinent subtleties. Utilize an expert and steady visual tasteful across the entirety of your web-based entertainment stages to make a firm and essential brand picture.

Then, decisively pick the substance you share on your web-based entertainment profiles to support your own image. Share content that features your skill, interests, and values, and offers some incentive to your crowd. Whether it's industry bits of knowledge, thought initiative articles, or in the background looks into your life, curate content that reverberates with your interest group and grandstands your remarkable point of view.

Moreover, draw in with your crowd consistently by answering remarks, messages, and notices in a convenient and bona fide way. Building certified associations and encouraging discussions via online entertainment reinforces your associations with your crowd as well as improves your image's perceivability and believability.

Also, influence the highlights and functionalities of every web-based entertainment stage to boost your image openness and commitment. Use hashtags, labeling, and geolocation elements to extend your compass and associate with similar people in your industry or specialty.

Ultimately, routinely screen and dissect your web-based entertainment measurements to keep tabs on your development and refine your procedure over the long run. Focus on key execution pointers, for example, adherent development, commitment rates, and content execution to recognize what resounds most with your crowd and change your methodology as needs be.

By upgrading your virtual entertainment profiles, you'll make major areas of strength for a significant internet based presence that really conveys your own image and draws in open doors lined up with your objectives and yearnings. In this section, we'll dive further into the techniques and best practices for advancing your online entertainment presence to upgrade your own marking endeavors and accomplish your ideal results.

Making Important Substance

In the computerized scene, quality writing is everything — and making significant, drawing in satisfied is fundamental for building serious areas of strength for a brand on the web. Whether it's blog entries, recordings, digital broadcasts, or virtual entertainment refreshes, your substance fills in as a vehicle for conveying your mastery, sharing your experiences, and interfacing with your crowd on a more profound level.

Begin by characterizing your substance system, illustrating the points, topics, and arrangements that line up with your own image and resound with your main interest group. Think about your interesting viewpoint, encounters, and mastery, and recognize the kinds of content that permit you to feature your assets and offer some benefit to your crowd.

Then, center around making great substance that is enlightening, important, and locking in. Offer viable tips, significant bits of knowledge, and provocative points of view that address your crowd's requirements, difficulties, and interests. Endeavor to be legitimate, straightforward, and engaging in your substance, sharing individual tales, stories, and encounters that resound with your crowd on a human level.

Besides, be reliable in your substance creation endeavors, keeping a normal presenting timetable and rhythm on make your crowd connected with and want more and more. Whether it's everyday blog refreshes, week after week recordings, or month to month bulletins, lay out a normal that works for yourself as well as your crowd, and stick to it.

Furthermore, influence mixed media configurations and channels to enhance your substance and contact a more extensive crowd. Explore different avenues regarding various arrangements, for example, infographics, online courses, live streams, and intuitive substance to keep your crowd connected with and amped up for your image.

Ultimately, energize communication and commitment with your substance by welcoming your crowd to like, remark, share, and take part in conversations. Answer expeditiously to remarks and messages, and cultivate a feeling of local area and having a place among your devotees.

By making significant substance that reverberates with your crowd and supports your own image, you'll secure yourself as a confided in expert in your specialty and draw in valuable open doors lined up with your objectives and desires. In this part, we'll dive further into the procedures and best practices for making convincing substance that raises your own marking endeavors and drives significant commitment with your crowd.

Drawing in with Your Crowd

Building areas of strength for a presence goes past communicating your message — it's tied in with cultivating certified associations and building associations with your crowd. Drawing in with your crowd improves your image's perceivability and validity as well as makes a feeling of local area and unwaveringness among your devotees.

Begin by effectively paying attention to your crowd and focusing on their requirements, inclinations, and criticism. Screen remarks, messages, and notices on your virtual entertainment profiles, blog entries, and other substance to comprehend what reverberates most with your crowd and how you can all the more likely serve them.

Then, answer instantly and truly to remarks, questions, and requests from your crowd. Recognize their commitments, address their interests, and offer thanks for their help and commitment. By drawing in with your crowd in a significant and certifiable manner, you'll construct trust, compatibility, and dedication after some time.

Additionally, start discussions and communications with your crowd to cultivate further associations and commitment. Suggest conversation starters, request criticism, and urge support in conversations to make a feeling of local area and coordinated effort around your image.

Furthermore, influence intuitive highlights and organizations via web-based entertainment stages to empower commitment and connection with your crowd. Have live back and forth discussions, surveys, challenges, and other intelligent occasions to ignite discussion and support interest from your devotees.

Moreover, consider teaming up with powerhouses, thought pioneers, or different brands in your industry to grow your range and draw in with new crowds. Banding together with similar people or associations can enhance your message and increment your image's perceivability and believability.

Finally, consistently assess and examine your crowd commitment measurements to keep tabs on your development and distinguish regions for development. Focus on measurements like preferences, remarks, offers, and navigate rates to check the adequacy of your commitment endeavors and change your technique as needs be.

By effectively captivating with your crowd, you'll encourage more grounded associations, increment brand faithfulness, and drive significant connections that add to the development and outcome of your own image. In this section, we'll investigate the systems and best practices for drawing in with your crowd online to augment your image's effect and impact.

Utilizing LinkedIn for Proficient Marking

LinkedIn stands apart as a strong stage for proficient systems administration and individual marking, offering a plenty of devices and highlights to grandstand your mastery, interface with industry companions, and position yourself as an idea chief in your field. Utilizing LinkedIn actually can fundamentally upgrade your expert image and entryways to new open doors.

Begin by upgrading your LinkedIn profile to successfully mirror your own image. Guarantee that your profile photograph is proficient and lines up with your image picture, and specialty a convincing title and rundown that plainly impart your offer and mastery. Modify your LinkedIn URL to incorporate your name or important catchphrases, making it more straightforward for others to find and interface with you.

Then, populate your LinkedIn profile with applicable data, including your work insight, instruction, abilities, and achievements. Feature key accomplishments, undertakings, and honors that show your aptitude and validity in your field. Use interactive media elements like recordings, introductions, and articles to exhibit your work and give extra setting to your profile guests.

Besides, effectively draw in with your LinkedIn network by sharing important substance, taking part in industry conversations, and associating with similar experts. Share wise articles, thought authority pieces, and industry experiences that exhibit your skill and offer some benefit to your crowd. Draw in with posts from your associations by loving, remarking, and sharing, and add to important LinkedIn gatherings and networks to extend your range and perceivability.

Furthermore, influence LinkedIn's distributing stage to distribute long-structure articles and thought authority pieces that lay out you as an educated authority in your field. Expound on points that are applicable to your crowd's advantages and difficulties, and give significant experiences and counsel that exhibit your mastery and validity.

Moreover, effectively search out and sustain associations with key powerhouses, thought pioneers, and chiefs in your industry. Associate with them on LinkedIn, draw in with their substance, and start significant discussions to construct affinity and lay out commonly valuable connections.

Finally, routinely screen and examine your LinkedIn measurements to follow your profile execution and commitment levels. Focus on measurements, for example, profile sees, association demands, and post commitment to check the adequacy of your LinkedIn methodology and make changes on a case by case basis.

By utilizing LinkedIn for proficient marking, you'll upgrade your perceivability, validity, and impact inside your industry and then some. In this part, we'll investigate the systems and best practices for boosting your effect on LinkedIn and utilizing the stage to propel your own marking objectives.

Dealing with Your Web-based Standing

In the present computerized age, your web-based standing assumes a basic part in forming how others see you and your own image. Overseeing and keeping a positive web-based standing is fundamental for building trust, validity, and authority in your industry or field.

Begin by directing a far reaching review of your web-based presence to survey your ongoing standing. Google yourself and audit the list items to see what data is promptly accessible about you on the web. Focus on both positive and negative substance, including news stories, virtual entertainment posts, audits, and notices.

Then, find proactive ways to address any negative or harming content that might be influencing your internet based standing. Assuming that you go over bad surveys or remarks, answer mindfully and expertly, addressing any worries or issues raised and looking to agreeably determine them. Moreover, consider connecting with the site or stage facilitating the negative substance to demand its expulsion or amendment, if proper.

In addition, effectively deal with your virtual entertainment profiles and online collaborations to guarantee they ponder decidedly your own image. Be aware of the substance you share and the remarks you make, and try not to take part in questionable or troublesome subjects that could discolor your standing. Routinely audit your security settings and safety efforts to safeguard your web-based character and limit the gamble of unapproved access or abuse of your own data.

Moreover, effectively search out chances to fabricate and advance positive substance that upgrades your internet based standing. Share examples of overcoming adversity, tributes, and supports from fulfilled clients or partners, and feature your ability through thought initiative articles, introductions, and talking commitment. By reliably exhibiting your impressive skill, mastery, and trustworthiness, you'll support your web-based standing and set up a good foundation for yourself as a confided in expert in your field.

Moreover, screen your web-based standing routinely utilizing instruments and administrations that track notices, audits, and other applicable substance connected with your own image. Set up Google Cautions for your name and applicable watchwords to remain informed about any new satisfied or makes reference to that might influence your standing. By remaining careful and proactive in dealing with your web-based standing, you can guarantee that your own image areas of strength for stays, and tough notwithstanding expected difficulties or debates.

In this part, we'll investigate the systems and best practices for dealing with your web-based standing successfully, giving viable tips and experiences to help you shield and upgrade your own image's picture and notoriety in the advanced world.

CHAPTER 4: NETWORKING AND RELATIONSHIP BUILDING

Understanding the Significance of Systems administration

Organizing is in many cases hailed as a foundation of individual and expert achievement, and for good explanation. At its center, organizing is tied in with building and sustaining associations with others, making a trap of associations that can open ways to potential open doors, backing, and development. Whether you're hoping to propel your profession, develop your business, or just extend your group of friends, organizing assumes a significant part in assisting you with accomplishing your objectives.

One of the critical advantages of systems administration is the entrance it gives to new open doors and assets. By interfacing with an assorted scope of people across various ventures, callings, and foundations, you gain openness to novel thoughts, viewpoints, and open doors that you might not have experienced in any case. Systems administration can prompt open positions, business organizations, mentorship connections, and important bits of knowledge that can impel your own and proficient development.

Besides, organizing offers a stage for sharing information, skill, and backing with others. By drawing in with similar people and specialists in your field, you can trade thoughts, look for counsel, and work together on undertakings or drives that benefit the two players. Organizing likewise offers a help organization of friends and tutors who can offer direction, support, and viewpoint during testing times.

Moreover, organizing assumes a urgent part in private marking and notoriety the executives. By developing areas of strength for an of associations, you upgrade your perceivability, believability, and impact inside your industry or local area. Your organization can act as a strong backer for your own image, underwriting your abilities, mastery, and character to other people.

Notwithstanding these unmistakable advantages, organizing likewise offers immaterial rewards like companionship, fellowship, and a feeling of having a place. Building significant associations with others can improve your life by and by and expertly, giving a feeling of local area and backing that upgrades your general prosperity.

In this part, we'll dive further into the significance of systems administration, investigating its heap advantages and offering functional tips and techniques for building and sustaining your organization actually. By understanding the meaning of systems administration and putting time and exertion into developing significant associations, you'll lay the basis for long haul achievement and satisfaction in both your own and proficient life.

Building Your Systems administration Methodology

Powerful systems administration requires more than basically going to occasions and trading business cards — it requires an essential methodology zeroed in on building certified associations and encouraging commonly useful connections. Fostering a systems administration methodology permits you to expand your time and endeavors, distinguish open doors lined up with your objectives, and develop areas of strength for a different organization of contacts.

Begin by laying out clear and explicit systems administration objectives that line up with your own and proficient goals. What do you expect to accomplish through systems administration? Is it safe to say that you are hoping to propel your vocation, extend your client base, or gain experiences into another industry? By characterizing your objectives forthright, you can tailor your systems administration endeavors to focus on open doors that line up with your needs and goals.

Then, distinguish your interest group and key contacts inside your organization. Who can assist you with accomplishing your systems administration objectives? Think about experts in your industry or field, thought pioneers, forces to be reckoned with, possible clients or clients, coaches, and friends. Make a rundown of target associations and focus on them in view of their importance and expected influence on your objectives.

Whenever you've recognized your interest group, investigate different systems administration channels and stages to associate with them. This might incorporate going to industry gatherings and occasions, joining proficient affiliations or systems administration gatherings, partaking in web-based discussions and networks, and utilizing online entertainment stages like LinkedIn. Pick organizing channels that line up with your inclinations, assets, and goals, and be proactive in starting and supporting associations with your objective contacts.

Also, center around better standards without compromise while building your organization. Rather than attempting to interface with whatever number individuals as could be expected under the circumstances, focus on building significant and bona fide associations with a select gathering of people who share your qualities, interests, and objectives. Put time and exertion into getting to know your contacts on a more profound level, figuring out their requirements, difficulties, and goals, and tracking down ways of enhancing their lives or professions.

Also, be key in your systems administration exercises, adjusting your time and assets between various channels and potential open doors. Put away committed time for systems administration exercises, whether it's going to occasions, contacting contacts, or circling back to associations. Be predictable and proactive in your systems administration endeavors, yet in addition be patient and tireless, as building significant connections takes time and exertion.

In this part, we'll investigate the most common way of building a key systems administration procedure, giving down to earth tips and bits of knowledge to assist you with boosting your systems administration endeavors and accomplish your own and proficient objectives. By fostering an unmistakable arrangement and way to deal with systems administration, you'll build your viability, grow your chances, and fabricate areas of strength for a steady organization that drives you towards progress.

Supporting Significant Connections

Building areas of strength for an isn't just about making associations — it's tied in with sustaining significant and legitimate associations with those associations over the long run. Certified connections are the groundwork of successful systems administration, giving a strong structure to cooperation, support, and shared development.

To support significant connections, begin by drawing nearer coordinating with a certified and bona fide outlook. Be earnest in your collaborations, showing a real premium in getting to know others and grasping their necessities, objectives, and difficulties. Credibility breeds trust and compatibility, laying the preparation for more profound and more significant associations.

Then, center around correspondence in your systems administration endeavors. Look for chances to enhance your associations' lives or vocations, whether it's by offering support, sharing experiences or assets, or making acquaintances with important contacts. By offering liberally without expecting anything as a trade off, you'll fabricate generosity and entrust with your organization, fortifying your connections after some time.

Additionally, focus on continuous correspondence and commitment with your organization. Keep in contact with your associations consistently, whether it's through messages, calls, virtual entertainment collaborations, or in-person gatherings. Share refreshes about your work, accomplishments, and interests, and show certified interest in your associations' lives and achievements. By remaining associated and drew in, you'll keep up with top-of-mind mindfulness with your organization and develop your connections after some time.

Furthermore, be proactive in offering backing and help to your associations when required. Be receptive to their solicitations for help or guidance, and deal your ability, assets, or associations whenever the situation allows. Go about as an asset and promoter for your associations, assisting them with exploring difficulties, jump all over chances, and accomplish their objectives.

Besides, look for valuable chances to team up and cooperate with your associations on ventures, drives, or occasions. Cooperative endeavors reinforce your connections as well as make an incentive for the two players, prompting shared accomplishment and development. Search for ways of utilizing each other's assets, mastery, and organizations to accomplish shared targets and make mutual benefit results.

In this part, we'll investigate the significance of sustaining significant connections in systems administration, giving useful hints and techniques to building solid and enduring associations with your organization. By cultivating certifiable connections based on trust, correspondence, and common help, you'll make a strong organization of partners and supporters who can assist you with accomplishing your own and proficient objectives.

Organizing Manners and Best Practices

Compelling systems administration isn't just about making associations — it's likewise about carefully maintaining impressive skill, kindness, and regard in the entirety of your communications. Organizing behavior envelops a bunch of rules and best practices that oversee how you draw in with others in systems administration settings, guaranteeing that you have a positive impression and fabricate significant associations with your contacts.

Most importantly, approach organizing occasions and collaborations with a positive and open outlook. Be well disposed, congenial, and inviting to other people, and endeavor to make a warm and comprehensive environment where everybody feels esteemed and regarded. Grin, visually connect, and offer a strong handshake while meeting new individuals, and utilize undivided attention methods to show veritable interest and commitment to the discussion.

Also, be aware of your non-verbal communication and non-verbal signs during systems administration associations. Keep up with open and welcoming non-verbal communication, for example, confronting the individual you're talking with, keeping up with great stance, and abstaining from folding your arms or seeming diverted. Focus on your manner of speaking and looks, conveying warmth, energy, and truthfulness in your cooperations.

Additionally, be aware of others' time and limits during systems administration occasions and cooperations. Abstain from hoarding discussions or intruding on others, and be aware of signs that show when now is the ideal time to wrap up a discussion or continue on toward the following individual. Regard individual space and limits, and keep away from meddling or excessively recognizable way of behaving that might make others anxious.

Moreover, practice great subsequent behavior in the wake of systems administration occasions or gatherings. Send customized cards to say thanks or messages to communicate your appreciation for the chance to interface and emphasize central issues from your discussion. Keep any word or responsibilities you made during the collaboration, like sending data or making presentations, promptly.

Finally, be proactive in sustaining and keeping up with your organization after some time. Keep in contact with your contacts consistently, whether it's through online entertainment, email, or in-person gatherings. Share important updates, articles, or assets that might bear some significance with your organization, and deal your help and help at whatever point required. By remaining connected with and proactive in your systems administration endeavors, you'll fortify your connections and expand the worth of your organization over the long run.

In this part, we'll investigate the standards of systems administration manners and best works on, giving reasonable tips and bits of knowledge to assist you explore organizing occasions and cooperations with impressive skill, graciousness, and certainty. By excelling at systems administration decorum, you'll have a positive impression, fabricate significant connections, and set out open doors for individual and expert development.

Utilizing Internet Systems administration Instruments

In the present advanced age, web based systems administration apparatuses and stages offer remarkable chances to associate with experts, grow your organization, and access important assets and bits of knowledge from anyplace on the planet. Utilizing these instruments really can essentially upgrade your systems administration endeavors and entryways to new open doors and joint efforts.

One of the most remarkable web based systems administration instruments is LinkedIn, an expert systems administration stage with more than 700 million clients around the

world. LinkedIn permits you to make a point by point profile displaying your expert experience, abilities, and achievements, and interface with experts in your industry or field.
Find opportunity to streamline your LinkedIn profile, including an expert photograph, a convincing title, and a definite
outline that features your mastery and offer.

Also, effectively draw in with your LinkedIn network by sharing important substance, partaking in bunch conversations,
and contacting associate with new contacts. Utilize LinkedIn's
hunt and proposal highlights to recognize and interface with
experts who share your inclinations, skill, or vocation objectives, and influence LinkedIn's informing and InMail elements
to start discussions and fabricate connections.

Notwithstanding LinkedIn, there are numerous other internet organizing stages and devices that can assist you with
growing your organization and interface with similar experts.
Proficient discussions, industry-explicit networks, and virtual
systems administration occasions offer chances to draw in
with peers, share bits of knowledge, and fabricate associations
with experts in your field. Investigate these stages and partake in conversations, clarify pressing issues, and proposition
your mastery to lay down a good foundation for yourself as a
significant individual from the local area.

In addition, influence web-based entertainment stages like
Twitter, Facebook, and Instagram to extend your internet
based presence and associate with experts beyond your nearby
organization. Share refreshes about your work, draw in with
industry powerhouses and thought pioneers, and take part in
significant discussions to build your perceivability and draw
in new associations.

Moreover, consider utilizing internet organizing apparatuses and stages to feature your skill and thoroughly considered authority writing for a blog, podcasting, or video content. Make and offer important substance that shows your insight, experiences, and viewpoints on points pertinent to your industry or field, and draw in with your crowd to encourage discussions and assemble connections.

In this part, we'll investigate the different web based systems administration apparatuses and stages accessible to experts, giving viable tips and procedures to utilizing these devices to grow your organization, fabricate connections, and advance your own and proficient objectives. By embracing web based systems administration apparatuses as a component of your systems administration methodology, you'll open new open doors for development, cooperation, and progress in your vocation.

CHAPTER 5: DEVELOPING YOUR EXPERTISE

Recognizing Your Specialized topics

Creating mastery starts with a reasonable comprehension of your assets, abilities, and information regions. Find opportunity to consider your expert encounters, scholastic foundation, and individual interests to recognize the regions where you succeed and have a profound comprehension. Think about the errands or ventures where you reliably perform well, get positive criticism, or exhibit a characteristic inclination.

Besides, look for input from associates, tutors, and companions to acquire experiences into your assets and regions for development. Request their viewpoint on your abilities, information, and commitments, and utilize their criticism to approve and refine your self-evaluation. Moreover, lead examination and assemble data about arising patterns, advances, and improvements in your industry or field to distinguish regions where you can develop your mastery and remain on the ball.

Besides, consider your drawn out profession objectives and desires while recognizing your specialized topics. Which jobs or positions do you try to in your profession? What abilities or information regions are fundamental for progress in those jobs? By adjusting your subject matters to your vocation objectives, you can zero in your endeavors on fostering the abilities and information that will drive you towards your ideal results.

In this part, we'll dig further into the most common way of distinguishing your subject matters, giving functional activities and procedures to assist you with acquiring lucidity and trust in your assets and capacities. By carving out opportunity to distinguish and use your subject matters, you'll establish the groundwork for turning into a perceived power and pioneer in your field.

Consistent Acquiring and Expertise Improvement

In the present quickly advancing world, mastery is definitely not a static state however a unique cycle that requires progressing mastering and expertise improvement. To develop mastery, it's vital for embrace an outlook of nonstop learning and a promise to extending your insight and leveling up your abilities all through your profession.

Begin by developing a hunger for information and an oddity about your field or industry. Remain informed about the most recent patterns, headways, and best practices through industry distributions, news sources, and expert improvement potential open doors. Search out learning open doors that line up with your inclinations and objectives, whether it's going to gatherings, studios, online classes, or signing up for online courses or affirmation programs.

Also, focus on ability improvement in regions that are applicable to your aptitude and profession goals. Recognize the vital abilities and capabilities that are sought after in your industry or field, and find proactive ways to obtain or improve those abilities. This might include searching out preparing or mentorship open doors, chipping in for testing projects, or seeking after high level training or accreditations.

Furthermore, embrace a development mentality that values trial and error, cycle, and gaining from disappointment. View mishaps and difficulties as any open doors for development and improvement, and move toward them with versatility, flexibility, and an eagerness to gain from your encounters. Embrace criticism as an important wellspring of understanding and direction, and use it to refine your abilities and work on your exhibition after some time.

Besides, influence innovation and computerized apparatuses to work with your mastering and expertise improvement venture. Exploit web based learning stages, instructive assets, and efficiency apparatuses to get to top notch content, team up with friends, and keep tabs on your development towards your learning objectives. Use virtual entertainment, gatherings, and online networks to associate with similar experts, share experiences, and trade thoughts and best practices.

In this section, we'll investigate the significance of ceaseless mastering and ability advancement in developing mastery, giving functional methodologies and assets to assist you with remaining on the ball and stay cutthroat in the present high speed world. By embracing a long lasting learning outlook and focusing on continuous expertise improvement, you'll situate yourself as a regarded power and pioneer in your field.

Thought Administration and Content Creation

Thought authority assumes an essential part in laying out skill and validity in your field. As an idea chief, you have the potential chance to share your remarkable experiences, viewpoints, and mastery with others, situating yourself as a confided in power and force to be reckoned with in your industry or specialty. Thought authority frequently remains closely connected with content creation, as it gives a stage to exhibiting your insight and thought initiative to a more extensive crowd.

Begin by distinguishing themes or regions where you have profound skill and an exceptional point of view to share. Consider your expert encounters, research interests, and industry patterns to distinguish significant and opportune points that reverberate with your interest group. Search for chances to offer new bits of knowledge, challenge the standard way of thinking, or give viable exhortation and answers for normal issues or difficulties in your field.

Then, influence different substance organizations and channels to make and share your thinking authority satisfied with your crowd. This might incorporate blog entries, articles, whitepapers, contextual investigations, recordings, webcasts, online courses, or virtual entertainment refreshes, contingent upon your inclinations and assets. Pick content arrangements that line up with your crowd's inclinations and utilization propensities, and analysis with various mediums to find what turns out best for you.

Additionally, center around making great substance that offers some benefit to your crowd and shows your aptitude and thought administration. Offer remarkable viewpoints, significant experiences, and down to earth guidance that address your crowd's necessities, difficulties, and desires. Be credible, straightforward, and engaging in your substance, sharing individual tales, stories, and guides to show your focuses and associate with your crowd on a human level.

Moreover, effectively draw in with your crowd and industry looks through your thinking authority content. Energize input, remarks, and conversations on your substance, and answer nicely and consciously to crowd requests and remarks. Partake in industry gatherings, gatherings, and occasions to impart your skill and experiences to a more extensive crowd and interface with similar experts.

Besides, consider teaming up with other idea pioneers, powerhouses, or associations in your field to enhance your compass and effect. Co-creating articles, facilitating joint online classes, or partaking in board conversations are only a couple of ways of utilizing the aggregate mastery and organizations of others to improve your thinking administration endeavors.

In this part, we'll investigate the standards of thought initiative and content creation, giving down to earth tips and systems to creating and sharing idea administration content that features your skill and lays out your believability as a forerunner in your field. By embracing thought initiative and making convincing substance, you'll situate yourself as a regarded power and powerhouse, driving significant effect and commitment inside your industry or specialty.

Building Validity and Authority

Believability and authority are fundamental parts of aptitude, molding how others see and trust your insight, abilities, and bits of knowledge. Building validity and authority requires a conscious and steady work to lay out a standing for mastery, impressive skill, and honesty in your field.

One method for building validity and authority is by acquiring significant experience and ability through involved work, research, or concentrated preparing. Search out chances to extend your insight and abilities in your subject matter, whether it's through hands on experience, high level training, or expert improvement programs. By exhibiting capability and capability in your field, you'll gain the trust and appreciation of your companions, associates, and clients.

Also, acquiring accreditations or certifications can additionally improve your believability and authority in your field. Consider seeking after accreditations or expert assignments that are perceived and regarded in your industry, as they act as substantial proof of your mastery and obligation to consistent learning and expert turn of events. Feature your accreditations and qualifications noticeably in your resume, LinkedIn profile, and other expert profiles to build up your validity and aptitude to other people.

Moreover, feature your aptitude and thoroughly considered administration public talking, composing, or educating commitment. Talking at meetings, studios, or industry occasions permits you to impart your insight and experiences to a more extensive crowd and lay down a good foundation for yourself as an informed authority. Additionally, composing articles, blog entries, or whitepapers on subjects applicable to your field exhibits your thinking initiative and ability to other people. Educating or tutoring others in your subject matter additionally hardens your validity and authority, as it expects you to verbalize your insight and guide others in their learning and improvement.

Besides, effectively look for chances to add to your industry or expert local area through humanitarian effort, council association, or positions of authority in proficient associations. By effectively partaking in industry drives and contributing your aptitude to aggregate endeavors, you'll improve your perceivability, believability, and impact inside your field.

In this section, we'll investigate systems for building validity and authority in your field, giving reasonable tips and experiences to assist you with laying out a standing as a confided in master and pioneer. By zeroing in on building validity and authority, you'll reinforce your own image and position yourself for progress in your profession.

Organizing with Industry Friends and Powerhouses

Organizing with industry companions and powerhouses is an important technique for extending your insight, acquiring experiences, and building connections that help your continuous improvement as a specialist. By associating with others in your field, you can get to new viewpoints, remain informed about industry drifts, and team up on ventures or drives that advance your mastery and vocation.

Begin by recognizing key people and associations in your industry or specialty that you appreciate and regard. These may incorporate idea pioneers, powerhouses, tutors, partners, or associations that are making critical commitments to your field. Utilize internet organizing stages, industry occasions, and expert relationship to associate with these people and begin building associations with them.

While systems administration with industry friends and powerhouses, move toward collaborations with a certifiable and real outlook. Try to lay out commonly advantageous connections in light of trust, regard, and shared interests. Carve out opportunity to find out about the work and achievements of your associations, and search for chances to give worth or backing to them as a trade off.

Also, effectively draw in with your organization by taking part in industry conversations, sharing bits of knowledge, and offering help or counsel when required. Contribute your ability and viewpoints to discussions and discussions, and be available to gaining from other people who have various encounters or perspectives. By effectively captivating with your organization, you'll exhibit your obligation to your field and position yourself as an important and regarded individual from the local area.

Also, search out potential chances to team up with industry companions and powerhouses on undertakings, exploration, or drives that line up with your skill and interests. Cooperative endeavors extend your organization as well as give potential chances to gain from others, trade thoughts, and make esteem together. Search for ways of utilizing each other's assets, assets, and organizations to accomplish shared objectives and targets.

Besides, remain informed about industry occasions, meetings, and systems administration amazing open doors where you can associate with industry companions and powerhouses face to face. Go to gatherings, studios, or systems administration occasions pertinent to your field, and make the most of chances to meet and connect with others in participation. Be proactive in starting discussions and building associations with new contacts, and circle back to them a short time later to keep up with the association.

In this part, we'll investigate the significance of systems administration with industry companions and powerhouses in fostering your aptitude, giving down to earth tips and procedures to building and sustaining connections that help your continuous development and improvement as a specialist. By systems administration with industry friends and power-houses, you'll grow your insight, gain important experiences, and fabricate serious areas of strength for an organization that upgrades your mastery and profession achievement.

CONCLUSION:

Recap of Central issues

As we close our excursion through "10 Moves toward a Strong Individual Brand: Stick Out and Succeed," it's fundamental to consider the central issues we've covered all through this book. We've investigated the essential standards of individual marking, stressing the significance of validness, clearness, and consistency in molding your image personality. We've examined the meaning of systems administration and relationship working in extending your organization, getting to valuable open doors, and acquiring support from companions and coaches. Furthermore, we've featured the worth of ceaseless mastering and ability advancement in developing aptitude and remaining cutthroat in the present quick moving world. In addition, we've dove into the systems for building believability and authority in your field, including acquiring significant experience, getting accreditations, and exhibiting your mastery through thought administration and content creation. By getting it and applying these central issues, you'll be exceptional to construct a strong individual brand, stand apart from the group, and prevail in your own and proficient undertakings.

Consider Self-awareness

As you arrive at the finish of this book, pause for a minute to consider your self-awareness venture. Think about how you might interpret individual marking, organizing, skill advancement, and believability building has developed all through the parts. Ponder the experiences you've acquired, the abilities you've obtained, and the significant advances you've taken to upgrade your own image and skill.

Ponder the difficulties you've experienced enroute and how you've defeated them. Consider the breakthrough moments and motivation that have powered your advancement, as well as the illustrations gained from mishaps and impediments. Perceive the development and change you've encountered because of your obligation to self-awareness and personal growth.

In addition, ponder the regions where you've taken critical steps and the regions where there is still space for development. Distinguish any holes in your insight or abilities that you might want to address pushing ahead, and put forth objectives for additional turn of events and improvement. Embrace the excursion of persistent development and advancement, realizing that individual and expert improvement is a long lasting pursuit.

At last, praise your accomplishments and recognize the headway you've made on your excursion towards building a strong individual brand and mastery. Perceive the worth of your extraordinary assets, abilities, and encounters, and embrace them as key resources in forming your personality and accomplishing your objectives. By thinking about your self-improvement and embracing the illustrations learned, you'll be better prepared to proceed with your excursion with lucidity, reason, and certainty.

Obligation to Proceeded with Development

As you finish up your investigation of individual marking and mastery advancement, reaffirming your obligation to proceeded with development and personal growth is urgent. Individual marking and skill are not static accomplishments but rather progressing processes that require commitment, determination, and an eagerness to adjust to change.

Focus on keeping a development outlook, embracing difficulties as any open doors for learning and development. Remain open to novel thoughts, viewpoints, and encounters that can extend your points of view and develop your aptitude. Be proactive in searching out open doors for development and advancement, whether it's through additional schooling, proficient preparation, or active experience.

Additionally, focus on taking care of oneself and prosperity as fundamental parts of your development process. Deal with your physical, mental, and close to home wellbeing, and establish a steady climate that encourages your own and proficient turn of events. Encircle yourself with positive impacts, look for help from coaches and companions, and focus on exercises that support your whole self.

Moreover, embrace a feeling of strength and versatility notwithstanding difficulties and misfortunes. Perceive that difficulties are a characteristic piece of the development interaction and use them as any open doors to learn, develop, and get to the next level. Develop the fortitude to step beyond your usual range of familiarity, proceed with potentially dangerous courses of action, and seek after new open doors that stretch your abilities and grow your points of view.

Moreover, remain associated with your own and proficient organizations, utilizing their help, direction, and consolation as you explore your development process. Share your objectives, desires, and difficulties with confided in guides and companions, and look for their recommendation and point of view when required. Work together with other people who share your interests and values, and cultivate connections that help your continuous turn of events and achievement.

All in all, focus on a long lasting excursion of development, self-revelation, and personal growth. Embrace the difficulties and potential open doors that come your direction, and remain consistent with your vision and values as you endeavor to fabricate a strong individual brand and mastery that separates you and drives you towards your objectives. With devotion, constancy, and a guarantee to proceeded with development, the opportunities for individual and expert achievement are boundless.

Strengthening and Certainty

As you consider your excursion through "10 Moves toward a Strong Individual Brand: Stick Out and Succeed," embrace a feeling of strengthening and trust in your capacities and potential. Perceive the novel qualities, abilities, and encounters that characterize you and put you aside from others. Trust in your capacities to shape your own image, develop ability, and accomplish your objectives.

Have confidence in yourself and your ability to have a beneficial outcome in your own and proficient life. Embrace your validness and distinction, realizing that your one of a kind viewpoint and voice will impact others and draw in valuable open doors to you. Stand tall in your convictions and values, and let them guide your activities and choices as you explore your excursion towards progress.

Besides, develop a mentality of confidence and strength notwithstanding difficulties and misfortunes. Perceive that misfortunes are brief obstructions that give open doors to development and learning. Trust in your capacity to beat affliction, adjust to change, and arise more grounded and stronger on the opposite side.

Moreover, encircle yourself with a steady organization of tutors, friends, and partners who trust in your true capacity and root for you enroute. Search out coaches who can offer direction, intelligence, and support as you seek after your objectives and goals. Construct associations with peers who share your interests and values, and commend each other's victories and achievements.

Moreover, take responsibility for individual brand and skill, and be deliberate about how you introduce yourself to the world. Make a convincing story that features your extraordinary assets, achievements, and goals. Be strong in imparting your story and vision to other people, and let your certainty and enthusiasm radiate through in all that you do.

All in all, embrace a feeling of strengthening and certainty as you set out on your excursion towards building a strong individual brand and skill. Trust in yourself and your capacities, and let your validness and energy guide you towards progress. With certainty, assurance, and a confidence in yourself, you have the ability to accomplish anything you put your energy into.

Source of inspiration

As you close the last section of "10 Moves toward a Strong Individual Brand: Stick Out and Succeed," now is the right time to transform reflection right into it. Take the information, experiences, and methodologies you've acquired from this book and apply them in your everyday existence with goal and reason.

In the first place, put forth unambiguous and quantifiable objectives for your own marking and skill improvement venture. Whether it's refining your image personality, growing your organization, or getting new abilities, obviously characterize what achievement resembles for yourself and make a guide for accomplishing your objectives.

Then, make noteworthy strides towards your objectives by executing the procedures and strategies illustrated in this book. Construct your own image by making a convincing story, refining your internet based presence, and exhibiting your mastery through thought initiative and content creation. Grow your organization by effectively captivating with industry friends and powerhouses, going to systems administration occasions, and searching out mentorship valuable open doors.

In addition, focus on constant acquiring and ability improvement to develop your aptitude and remain on the ball in your field. Put resources into proficient advancement amazing open doors, search out tutors and mentors, and remain informed about arising patterns and best practices in your industry.

Also, center around building believability and authority in your field by acquiring important experience, getting accreditations, and effectively adding to your industry or expert local area. Set up a good foundation for yourself as a confided in master and thoroughly considered pioneer your activities, words, and commitments to your field.

Moreover, recall that individual marking and skill advancement are progressing processes that require commitment, diligence, and versatility. Remain focused on your development process, and turn, repeat, and course-right on a case by case basis enroute.

All in all, jump all over the chance to take your own marking and aptitude improvement to a higher level by placing the experiences and systems from this book into training. Earnestly, center, and a pledge to nonstop improvement, you have the ability to make a strong individual brand, stand apart from the group, and accomplish your most out of this world fantasies. So go forward with certainty, and leave behind a legacy!